ACTIVATE YOUR GROWTH MINDSET TO TRANSFORM THOUGHTS OF SCARCITY INTO ABUNDANT OPPORTUNITIES

Easy Steps Women Can Take To Embrace Positive Circumstance As A Way Of Life

Practice gratitude: Focus on what you have instead of what you lack.

In a world that constantly tells us we don't have enough—enough money, success, time, or even love—it's easy to fall into the trap of a scarcity mindset. This mindset, rooted in the belief that there is a limited amount of everything, often leads to feelings of inadequacy, stress, and frustration. It's a mental state that can prevent us from fully appreciating the abundance that already exists in our lives.

One powerful antidote to this way of thinking is the practice of gratitude, which helps shift focus from what we lack to what we already have. When we cultivate gratitude, we train our minds to recognize the positive aspects of life, allowing us to escape the cycle of scarcity thinking and move toward a more fulfilling and abundant existence.

Understanding the Scarcity Mindset

At its core, the scarcity mindset is a psychological phenomenon that emphasizes limitation and lack. It's the feeling that resources—whether material, emotional, or relational—are finite, and there's never enough to go around. This mindset often leads to anxiety, competition, and comparison. When you believe you don't have enough, it's easy to become consumed with thoughts of deficiency, worrying about how to acquire more of what you think you lack.

The scarcity mindset can manifest in different ways. For some, it shows up in financial worries, the constant fear that money will run out, regardless of actual circumstances. For others, it might be a lack of self-worth, believing that they are never good enough, despite their accomplishments. In relationships, scarcity can lead to fear of abandonment, jealousy, or the belief that love and connection are limited resources.

The Power of Gratitude

Gratitude is a state of being that allows us to appreciate the good in our lives. It's a conscious acknowledgment of the things we value—whether they're material possessions, relationships, experiences, or personal qualities. When we practice gratitude, we intentionally shift our attention away from what's missing and instead focus on what we already have. This mindset not only boosts mental and emotional well-being but also fosters a sense of abundance.

Research has shown that gratitude can have profound effects on our mental health. According to a study published in the *Journal of Personality and Social Psychology*, individuals who regularly practice gratitude report higher levels of happiness, optimism, and life satisfaction. They are also less likely to experience negative emotions like envy, resentment, or regret. When we train our brains to look for the good in life, we reduce the influence of scarcity thinking and cultivate a more positive, abundant mindset.

Shifting Focus to What You Have

Practicing gratitude doesn't mean ignoring challenges or pretending that everything is perfect. Rather, it involves consciously shifting your perspective to focus on the positives, even when life feels difficult. This shift in focus helps reduce the anxiety and fear that come with the scarcity mindset.

Here are a few ways to cultivate gratitude and focus on what you have:

1. Start a Gratitude Journal

One of the most effective ways to practice gratitude is by keeping a gratitude journal. Each day, write down three to five things you are grateful for. These can be simple, everyday things like a warm cup of coffee, a supportive friend, or a moment of peace. Over time, this practice trains your brain to notice the good in your life, making it easier to shift away from thoughts of scarcity.

2. Practice Mindful Appreciation

Throughout the day, take moments to pause and mindfully appreciate what you have. This could be as simple as savoring a meal, enjoying the comfort of your home, or recognizing the love and support of friends and family. Mindfulness helps ground you in the present moment, making it easier to see the abundance around you.

3. Express Gratitude to Others

Take time to thank the people in your life who have made a positive impact, no matter how small. This could be a kind word to a coworker, a heartfelt message to a friend, or a note of appreciation to a family member. Expressing gratitude not only strengthens relationships but also reinforces your awareness of the positive influences in your life.

4. Reframe Negative Thoughts

When you catch yourself thinking in terms of scarcity— whether it's about money, time, or personal success—

try to reframe those thoughts in a more positive light. For example, instead of focusing on what you haven't achieved, remind yourself of what you've already accomplished. Instead of worrying about not having enough time, reflect on how you can make the most of the time you do have.

5. Set Intentions Based on Abundance

Goal-setting is important, but it's essential to set intentions from a place of abundance rather than lack. When you set goals with a scarcity mindset, you may feel pressured to achieve them out of fear or desperation. Instead, set goals that reflect your strengths and the opportunities available to you. This shift in mindset allows you to approach your aspirations with optimism and enthusiasm.

The Benefits of Gratitude in Combating Scarcity

Gratitude does more than just make us feel good in the moment; it rewires our brains to think differently. Studies show that practicing gratitude can increase dopamine and serotonin, the brain chemicals responsible for happiness and well-being. Over time, this rewiring helps us break free from the constant cycle of scarcity thinking, allowing us to develop a more positive outlook on life.

Focusing on what you have also helps combat the comparison trap, a key feature of the scarcity mindset. In today's world, it's easy to compare ourselves to others—whether it's their social status, financial success, or personal achievements. When we practice gratitude, we stop comparing ourselves to others and instead appreciate our unique journey. This shift reduces feelings of inadequacy and promotes a sense of contentment.

Additionally, gratitude fosters resilience. Life inevitably presents challenges, but when you practice gratitude, you're better equipped to handle setbacks with grace. Instead of dwelling on what's wrong, you can find strength in what's going well, allowing you to navigate difficulties with a more balanced perspective.

Conclusion

Breaking free from a scarcity mindset requires intentional practice, and gratitude is one of the most powerful tools in this journey. By focusing on what you have rather than what you lack, you can shift your mindset from one of limitation to one of abundance. Gratitude helps you appreciate the present, strengthen relationships, and foster a more positive outlook on life.

Over time, this practice can rewire your brain, making it easier to navigate life's challenges with a sense of abundance and fulfillment.

In a world that often encourages us to focus on scarcity, gratitude is a revolutionary act—one that can transform not only your perspective but your entire life.

Surround Yourself with Positivity: People with an Abundance Mindset can help uplift your Perspective.

In a world where competition, comparison, and pressure to "keep up" are prevalent, many of us can fall into the trap of a scarcity mindset. This mentality makes us believe that there is a limited amount of success, happiness, or fulfillment available, leading to feelings of inadequacy, fear, and anxiety.

However, one of the most powerful ways to combat this mindset is by surrounding yourself with people who embody an abundance mindset— those who focus on possibilities, opportunities, and optimism. These individuals have the capacity to uplift your perspective, encourage your growth, and help you move beyond scarcity thinking to live a more fulfilling, empowered life.

Understanding the Abundance vs. Scarcity Mindset

Before exploring how to surround yourself with positivity, it's essential to understand the difference between an abundance mindset and a scarcity mindset.

A scarcity mindset is rooted in the belief that life offers limited opportunities, resources, or happiness. People with this mindset often focus on what they don't have, whether it's wealth, success, or relationships. They may feel threatened by others' achievements and worry that there isn't enough room for everyone to succeed. As a result, they may hold back, avoid taking risks, or feel stuck in a cycle of fear and comparison.

Conversely, an abundance mindset is grounded in the belief that there is plenty to go around. People with this mindset see the world as full of opportunities and potential. They understand that someone else's success doesn't diminish their own, and they are open to collaboration, growth, and learning. They radiate positivity, approach challenges with optimism, and focus on long-term solutions rather than short-term fears.

Surrounding yourself with individuals who possess this kind of mindset can help shift your perspective and inspire you to adopt similar beliefs. Here's how surrounding yourself with positivity can transform your life.

The Impact of the People You Surround Yourself With

The saying "you are the average of the five people you spend the most time with" rings true when it comes to mindset and outlook on life. The people in your immediate circle have a significant influence on your thoughts, attitudes, and behaviors. If you consistently interact with people who focus on lack and limitations, their scarcity mindset may begin to seep into your own thinking. On the other hand, when you spend time with individuals who embrace positivity, growth, and abundance, you're more likely to adopt those traits yourself.

Being in the presence of positive, uplifting individuals can provide several key benefits:

1. Inspiration and Motivation

People with an abundance mindset tend to inspire those around them. They see challenges as opportunities and setbacks as lessons. By surrounding yourself with individuals who are driven, optimistic, and solution-oriented, you'll find yourself feeling more motivated to pursue your own goals. Their energy can ignite your own ambition, encouraging you to focus on possibilities instead of limitations.

2. Support and Encouragement

When you surround yourself with positive people, you gain a network of support. Abundance-minded individuals are typically generous with their time, resources, and encouragement. They're willing to help others succeed because they believe that there is enough success for everyone. This type of support system can boost your confidence and help you overcome self-doubt, especially during challenging times.

3. Shift in Perspective

Scarcity thinking often leads to tunnel vision, where you become fixated on what you lack or fear. In contrast, people with an abundance mindset see life through a lens of possibility. They're able to identify opportunities that others may overlook. By spending time with these individuals, you'll begin to see life from a broader perspective, learning to recognize and appreciate the opportunities that exist around you.

4. Collaborative Spirit

Abundance-minded people are often collaborative rather than competitive. They understand that working together can create more value for everyone involved. When you surround yourself with individuals who have this collaborative spirit, you're more likely to seek out partnerships, share ideas, and contribute to others' success without fear of losing out. This mindset fosters a sense of community and mutual growth.

5. Emotional Well-Being

Positive, abundance-minded people tend to have a contagious sense of optimism and joy. Their positive energy can uplift your mood, reduce stress, and enhance your overall emotional well-being. When you regularly engage with individuals who focus on gratitude, possibility, and personal growth, their attitudes will naturally rub off on you, helping you maintain a healthier, more balanced outlook on life.

How to Surround Yourself with Positivity

If you recognize that the people in your current circle are contributing to a scarcity mindset, it's important to take intentional steps to surround yourself with more positive influences. Here are a few ways to do so:

1. Seek Out Mentors

Look for mentors who embody the abundance mindset. These individuals can provide guidance, encouragement, and insights that can help you shift your own thinking. Whether they're leaders in your field, successful entrepreneurs, or individuals who radiate positivity, mentors can offer valuable perspectives that challenge your limiting beliefs.

2. Join Like-Minded Communities

Participating in groups, clubs, or online communities that promote growth, positivity, and abundance can help you connect with like-minded individuals. Whether it's a professional network, a mastermind group, or a social circle centered around personal development, surrounding yourself with people who share similar values can reinforce your commitment to cultivating an abundance mindset.

3. Distance Yourself from Negative Influences

While it may be difficult, it's important to distance yourself from individuals who consistently project negativity, fear, or limitation. If certain relationships drain your energy or reinforce scarcity thinking, consider setting boundaries. This doesn't mean cutting people out of your life completely, but rather, minimizing your exposure to their limiting beliefs while focusing on your own growth.

4. Engage with Positive Content

The media, books, and content you consume also play a significant role in shaping your mindset. Surround yourself with positive, empowering content that reinforces an abundance mindset. Read books on personal growth, listen to podcasts that inspire optimism, and engage with social media accounts that promote positivity and possibility.

5. Practice Gratitude with Others

Gratitude is a cornerstone of the abundance mindset. Surround yourself with people who actively practice gratitude and share this practice with them. Whether it's through conversations, gratitude journals, or social media posts, engaging in regular gratitude with others helps strengthen your focus on what's going right in your life rather than what's missing.

Conclusion

The company you keep can either reinforce a scarcity mindset or help you cultivate an abundance mindset. By surrounding yourself with individuals who embrace positivity, growth, and collaboration, you create an environment that fosters your own personal development. These positive influences can inspire, uplift, and encourage you to see the world as full of possibilities, helping you break free from the limiting beliefs of scarcity thinking.

Ultimately, the journey toward abundance requires intentional action and the support of a community that shares your values. Surround yourself with people who believe in abundance, and watch as their positive energy transforms your own mindset, leading to a more fulfilling and empowered life.

Acknowledge Your Scarcity Mindset: Recognize That You Have A Scarcity Mindset And Consider The Thoughts That Are Causing It.

Let's take a moment to recognize that a scarcity mindset is a psychological trap that affects many people at different points in life. By recognizing and understanding the thoughts that fuel this mindset and exploring their origins, you can begin to cultivate a healthier, more abundant perspective.

What is a Scarcity Mindset?

Before diving into how to acknowledge and address your scarcity mindset, it's essential to understand what it is. A scarcity mindset focuses on limitations and deficits. People with this mindset are

constantly preoccupied with what they don't have—
whether it's material possessions, personal
achievements, or emotional fulfillment. There is a
chronic belief that there is never enough—whether
it's money, success, time, love, or opportunities.

This perception often leads to feelings of fear,
anxiety, anger, and competition, causing people to
focus on what they lack rather than what they have.
This mentality can lead to negative behaviors such
as comparison (comparison is the thief of joy), fear
of missing out (FOMO), and hoarding resources—
either emotionally or financially.

A scarcity mindset can also manifest as self-doubt.
You may find yourself thinking that you're not good
enough, smart enough, or deserving of success.
This can affect various aspects of your life, from
your career and finances to your relationships and
personal growth. Left unchecked, it can create a
cycle where you overwork yourself to achieve but
no matter how much you achieve, you believe it will

never be enough. This reinforces feelings of inadequacy and fear.

Step 1: Recognize the Signs of a Scarcity Mindset

Acknowledging your scarcity mindset begins with self-awareness. To combat this mentality, you first need to recognize when and how it shows up in your thoughts and behaviors. Here are some common signs that you may be operating from a place of scarcity:

1. Constant Worry About Money or Resources

You may frequently worry about not having enough money or resources, even when your situation is relatively stable. This often manifests as anxiety about the future, fear of losing what you have, or an overwhelming sense that you'll never be able to afford the things you want or need.

2. Fear of Failure or Rejection

A scarcity mindset often leads to fear of taking risks. If you constantly worry about failure or rejection, it may be because you believe that there aren't enough opportunities to go around. This fear can prevent you from pursuing your goals or stepping outside your comfort zone, leading to stagnation.

3. Comparison and Envy

If you frequently compare yourself to others and feel envious of their achievements or possessions, this is a clear indication of a scarcity mindset. You may feel as though others' successes somehow diminish your own, or that their happiness is a threat to your potential for happiness.

4. Reluctance to Share or Give

People with a scarcity mindset are often hesitant to share their time, resources, or knowledge with others. This reluctance stems from the fear that helping others will leave them with less. Instead of viewing generosity as an opportunity to connect and grow, they see it as a zero-sum game.

5. Procrastination and Perfectionism

Scarcity thinking can fuel procrastination and perfectionism, as you may feel that you need to wait for the "perfect" time, opportunity, or circumstances before taking action. This belief that conditions must be ideal before you move forward can hold you back from making progress.

Step 2: Identify the Thoughts Fueling Your Scarcity Mindset

Once you recognize the signs of a scarcity mindset, the next step is to examine the specific thoughts that are driving it. By understanding the mental narratives that contribute to scarcity thinking, you can begin to challenge and reframe them. Here are some common scarcity-related thoughts and beliefs:

- "I'll never have enough money."

This belief often stems from a fear of financial instability or a lack of control over your financial situation. You may believe that no matter how hard you work or how much you save, you'll never feel secure or satisfied.

- "There aren't enough opportunities for me to succeed."

This thought reflects a belief that success is a limited resource. You may feel that because others are achieving their goals, there's less room for you to achieve yours.

- "I'm not good enough to deserve this."

Self-worth plays a significant role in a scarcity mindset. If you believe that you're not good enough, smart enough, or talented enough to deserve success or happiness, this can perpetuate a cycle of self-doubt and insecurity.

- "If I give to others, I'll have less for myself."

This belief is rooted in fear and competition. Whether it's sharing your time, energy, or resources, you may feel that giving to others will deplete what little you have, leaving you with nothing.

Step 3: Explore the Origins of Your Scarcity Mindset

To fully address your scarcity mindset, it's important to explore where these limiting beliefs originated. Often, they are rooted in past experiences, upbringing, culture or societal conditioning. Here are some common sources of scarcity thinking:

1. Family and Upbringing

Your childhood environment plays a crucial role in shaping your mindset. If you grew up in a household where resources were limited, or where there was a constant focus on saving money and avoiding risks, these messages may have imprinted deeply. Even if your financial situation has improved, you may still carry the fear and caution from your early experiences.

2. Cultural and Societal Influences

Society often reinforces scarcity thinking through messages that equate success with material wealth and social status. The pressure to "keep up with the Joneses" can lead to feelings of inadequacy and a belief that you're falling behind if you don't have certain possessions, achievements, or experiences.

3. Past Failures or Setbacks

If you've experienced significant setbacks, such as a job loss, financial difficulties, or failed relationships, these events can contribute to a scarcity mindset. You may fear that history will repeat itself and that no matter how much effort you put in, things won't work out.

Your self-esteem and self-worth also play a significant role in scarcity thinking. If you struggle with self-doubt or feelings of inadequacy, it can be difficult to believe that you are deserving of success, happiness, or abundance.

Step 4: Challenge and Reframe Your Scarcity Thoughts

Once you've identified the thoughts and origins of your scarcity mindset, the next step is to challenge and reframe them. Begin by asking yourself whether these beliefs are truly based on reality or if they're distorted by fear and insecurity. For example, is it true that you'll never have enough money, or is this fear based on past experiences that no longer apply? Is it possible that there are more opportunities available to you than you initially thought?

Reframing scarcity thoughts involves shifting your focus from lack to abundance. Instead of thinking, "There aren't enough opportunities," reframe it as, "Opportunities are constantly emerging, and I can create my own path to success." By practicing gratitude, mindfulness, and positive self-affirmation, you can gradually rewire your brain to adopt a more abundant mindset.

Conclusion

Acknowledging and recognizing your scarcity mindset is a powerful step toward personal growth and fulfillment. By identifying the thoughts that fuel scarcity thinking and exploring their origins, you can begin to challenge and reframe these limiting beliefs. With consistent effort, you can shift your perspective from one of lack and limitation to one of abundance and possibility, ultimately leading to a more empowered and fulfilling life.

Choose Your Thoughts Intentionally: Question Whether Your Thoughts Are True And If There Is Evidence To Support Them.

Our thoughts shape the way we view and experience the world. When caught in a scarcity mindset, thoughts often revolve around lack, limitation, and fear—fear of not having enough time, money, love, or success. This way of thinking can cause stress, anxiety, and even self-sabotage. However, by choosing your thoughts intentionally and learning to question whether they are true or helpful, you can break free from the limitations of a scarcity mindset and begin to see the world through a lens of abundance.

Choosing your thoughts is a powerful skill that requires self-awareness and practice. It means recognizing that not every thought that enters your mind is accurate, helpful, or aligned with your goals. By becoming more intentional about which thoughts you entertain and which you challenge, you can reframe negative patterns and cultivate a healthier, more productive mindset.

The Power of Thoughts

Our thoughts create our reality. The way we think about ourselves, our circumstances, and the world around us directly impacts how we feel and what actions we take. When we consistently entertain thoughts of scarcity—such as "I'll never have enough money" or "I'm not good enough to succeed"—we reinforce those beliefs and create a self-fulfilling prophecy.

A scarcity mindset doesn't just limit what we believe is possible; it also influences our behavior.

When we focus on what we don't have, we may act out of fear, holding back from opportunities, avoiding risks, or hoarding resources. This reactive behavior can keep us stuck in a cycle of lack, unable to see the possibilities for growth and abundance.

In contrast, an abundance mindset encourages us to see opportunities rather than limitations. It helps us believe that there is enough success, love, time, and resources to go around, and that we are capable of creating positive outcomes in our lives. The first step to cultivating this mindset is to become intentional about the thoughts we choose to believe.

Step 1: Recognize Your Automatic Thoughts

The first step in choosing your thoughts intentionally is becoming aware of the automatic thoughts that run through your mind. Automatic

thoughts are the initial, unfiltered reactions we have
to situations—often shaped by past experiences,
fears, and subconscious beliefs. In many cases,
these thoughts are negative or fear-based,
especially when rooted in a scarcity mindset.

For example, if you're facing a challenging situation
at work, your automatic thought might be, "I'm not
smart enough to handle this," or "What if I fail?" If
you're struggling financially, you might think, "I'll
never get out of debt," or "I'll never be able to afford
the life I want."

These automatic thoughts often go unquestioned,
but they hold significant power over your mood and
behavior. The key is to recognize them when they
arise and challenge their validity.

Step 2: Question the Truth of Your Thoughts

Once you've identified an automatic thought, the next step is to ask yourself whether it's true. Often, negative or scarcity-driven thoughts are based on assumptions, fears, or distortions of reality, rather than factual evidence. Asking yourself questions like the following can help you challenge the accuracy of your thoughts:

- Is this thought based on fact, or is it based on fear?

- What evidence do I have to support this thought?

- Am I jumping to conclusions or making assumptions?

- Have I overcome similar challenges in the past?

- What would I say to a friend if they were having this thought?

For example, let's say you have the thought, "I'll never get out of debt." Is this thought true? You might realize that it's not—while you may be facing financial challenges, it's not necessarily true that you'll never be able to improve your situation. You might also recognize that this thought is rooted in fear rather than fact, and that you have taken steps in the past to manage your finances successfully, even if progress has been slow.

By questioning your thoughts in this way, you create space to challenge and reframe them, rather than accepting them as absolute truth.

Step 3: Look for Alternative Perspectives

After questioning the validity of a scarcity-driven thought, the next step is to look for alternative perspectives. This doesn't mean ignoring challenges or pretending that everything is perfect, but rather finding more balanced, constructive ways of thinking.

For example, instead of thinking, "I'll never get out of debt," you might reframe the thought to, "My financial situation is challenging right now, but I'm taking steps to improve it," or "I've overcome financial challenges in the past, and I can continue to make progress."

Similarly, if your automatic thought is, "I'm not good enough to succeed," you might challenge this by reminding yourself of your past achievements and strengths. Reframing this thought could sound like, "I may not have all the answers right now, but I'm capable of learning and growing."

The goal is to replace scarcity-driven thoughts with more balanced and empowering perspectives—

ones that acknowledge both the challenges and the possibilities.

Step 4: Practice Gratitude and Abundance Thinking

One of the most effective ways to shift from a scarcity mindset to an abundance mindset is by practicing gratitude. When you focus on what you're grateful for, you train your brain to recognize the positive aspects of your life, rather than fixating on what's missing. This shift in focus can help you develop a greater sense of abundance, even in challenging times.

Each day, take a few moments to reflect on what you're grateful for. This could include material things, such as your home or job, as well as relationships, experiences, or personal qualities. The more you practice gratitude, the more you'll begin to notice the abundance that already exists in your life.

Additionally, adopt abundance-oriented thinking by reminding yourself that opportunities are always available and that setbacks are temporary. For example, instead of thinking, "I missed my chance," reframe it as, "There will be more opportunities in the future."

Step 5: Take Action Based on Empowering Thoughts

Finally, it's important to act in alignment with the empowering thoughts you choose. Once you've reframed a scarcity-driven thought into a more positive perspective, ask yourself what actions you can take that reflect this new mindset.

For example, if you've reframed "I'll never get out of debt" into "I'm taking steps to improve my financial situation," you might take action by creating a budget, setting up a savings plan, or consulting with a financial advisor. These actions reinforce the belief that you are capable of improving your circumstances, further weakening the power of the scarcity mindset.

Similarly, if you've challenged the thought "I'm not good enough to succeed," you might take action by pursuing a new learning opportunity, seeking mentorship, or setting small, achievable goals to build confidence in your abilities.

Conclusion

Choosing your thoughts intentionally is a powerful way to combat a scarcity mindset and cultivate an abundance mentality. By recognizing automatic thoughts, questioning their truth, and reframing them into more balanced and empowering perspectives, you can break free from the limitations of scarcity thinking. Coupled with practices like gratitude and taking aligned action, this approach can help you create a life of greater abundance, possibility, and fulfillment.

Focus On Growth: Instead Of Focusing On What You Don't Have, Focus On Taking Action And Growing.

When you are constantly worried about what you don't have—whether it's money, opportunities, skills, or time—a scarcity mindset can have you feeling paralyzed, unable to move forward and achieve your goals. However, by shifting your focus from what is missing in your life to how you can **grow** and take action (a growth mindset), you can combat scarcity and cultivate an attitude of abundance and possibility.

Growth-oriented thinking helps individuals expand their capacity for success, learning, and personal development. Instead of seeing challenges as insurmountable obstacles, people who focus on growth view them as opportunities to improve and move closer to their goals. This shift in perspective not only helps to break the negative cycle of scarcity thinking but also empowers individuals to take action and create meaningful change in their lives.

The Limitations of a Scarcity Mindset

Before delving into how to focus on growth, it's important to understand how a scarcity mindset holds you back. A scarcity mindset is rooted in the belief that there is never enough—whether it's time, money, opportunities, or success. People with a scarcity mindset often feel that they are constantly competing for limited resources and that someone else's success diminishes their own chances for success.

This mentality can lead to a variety of negative outcomes, including:

- Fear of Failure: A scarcity mindset makes failure feel catastrophic. If you believe there aren't enough opportunities to go around, the thought of failing can lead to anxiety and a reluctance to take risks. You might avoid pursuing your goals altogether for fear that one failure will set you back indefinitely.

- Comparison and Envy: When you are focused on scarcity, it's easy to fall into the trap of comparing yourself to others. You might feel envious of their success, believing that their accomplishments mean there's less available for you. This can create feelings of inadequacy and dissatisfaction with your own life.

- Stagnation: A scarcity mindset can lead to stagnation because you may be too focused on preserving what little you believe you have, rather than taking bold steps to grow and improve. You may avoid new opportunities, resist change, or struggle to make progress toward your goals.

Shifting Focus: From Scarcity to Growth

To combat a scarcity mindset, it's crucial to shift your focus from what you lack to how you can grow. Instead of obsessing over the things you don't have, concentrate on the steps you can take to develop your skills, expand your knowledge, and improve your situation. This growth-oriented mindset allows you to see challenges as learning opportunities and view the future with optimism and possibility.

Step 1: Adopt a Growth Mindset

The concept of a growth mindset, popularized by psychologist Carol Dweck, is foundational to overcoming a scarcity mentality. A growth mindset is the belief that your abilities and intelligence can be developed through effort, learning, and perseverance. In contrast, a fixed mindset—often associated with scarcity thinking—holds that your talents and abilities are innate and unchangeable.

When you have a growth mindset, you see challenges as opportunities to learn and grow, rather than threats to your success. You understand that failure is a natural part of the growth process and that setbacks are temporary and surmountable.

To adopt a growth mindset, begin by embracing the idea that you are capable of improvement. Instead of viewing obstacles as barriers, see them as opportunities to develop new skills, gain experience, and become more resilient. Acknowledge that the path to success is often non-linear and that progress takes time and effort.

One of the most effective ways to combat a scarcity mindset is to focus on taking action rather than dwelling on what you don't have. When you are stuck in scarcity thinking, it's easy to feel overwhelmed by the gap between where you are and where you want to be. This focus on lack can lead to paralysis, making it difficult to take meaningful steps toward your goals.

Instead of fixating on what's missing, shift your attention to what you can do right now to improve your situation. Break down your goals into manageable steps and start taking action, even if those steps seem small at first. Every action you take moves you closer to growth and away from scarcity.

For example, if you're worried about not having enough money, instead of focusing on your financial limitations, ask yourself what actions you can take to improve your financial situation. This might include creating a budget, seeking additional income streams, or investing in learning new skills that can increase your earning potential. By focusing on action, you'll feel more empowered and less restricted by scarcity.

Step 3: Embrace Continuous Learning

Growth is not a destination; **it's a lifelong process**. To combat scarcity thinking, it's important to embrace continuous learning and see every experience—whether it's a success or a failure—as an opportunity to grow.

Invest in your personal and professional development by seeking out new knowledge, skills, and experiences. Read books, take courses, attend workshops, and surround yourself with people who inspire you to improve. When you adopt a mindset of continuous learning, you begin to see the world as full of opportunities for growth, rather than a place of limited resources.

By focusing on learning and self-improvement, you can overcome the fear that often accompanies a scarcity mindset. Instead of worrying about whether you have enough, you'll recognize that you are constantly growing, developing, and creating new opportunities for yourself.

Step 4: Set Growth-Oriented Goals

Another powerful way to shift from scarcity thinking to a growth mindset is to set goals that focus on your development rather than on external outcomes. Instead of setting goals that are based solely on acquiring material things or reaching certain milestones, create goals that are centered on personal growth and improvement.

For example, rather than setting a goal to earn a specific amount of money, set a goal to develop a new skill that can increase your earning potential. Rather than aiming to reach a certain level of success in your career, set a goal to learn something new each day that will make you a better professional. By focusing on growth-oriented goals, you can take action toward becoming the person you want to be, rather than fixating on what you don't have.

These types of goals are empowering because they put the emphasis on things you can control—your actions, your learning, and your development. When you focus on growth, external success will often follow naturally.

Step 5: Reframe Setbacks as Learning Opportunities

One of the most detrimental aspects of a scarcity mindset is the fear of failure. When you believe that resources are limited, failure can feel like a permanent setback. However, a growth mindset reframes failure as an essential part of the learning process.

Instead of viewing setbacks as proof that you're not good enough or that success is out of reach, reframe them as valuable learning experiences. Each failure brings with it lessons that can help you grow and improve in the future. The key is to remain resilient, learn from your mistakes, and use those lessons to move forward.

For example, if you experience a setback in your career, instead of viewing it as a sign that you're not capable, ask yourself what you can learn from the experience. What skills or strategies can you develop to avoid similar setbacks in the future? This growth-oriented approach helps you see challenges as temporary and surmountable, rather than as insurmountable obstacles.

Conclusion

Focusing on growth rather than scarcity is a powerful way to combat the limitations of a scarcity mindset. By adopting a growth mindset, taking action, embracing continuous learning, setting growth-oriented goals, and reframing setbacks as learning opportunities, you can shift your perspective from one of lack to one of abundance and possibility.

When you focus on your capacity to grow and improve, you empower yourself to create the life you want, regardless of external circumstances. Instead of being paralyzed by fear and scarcity, you'll be motivated by the endless opportunities for growth and personal development that are available to you.

Practice Mindfulness: Catch Time-Wasting Habits And Schedule Focused Times To Complete Them.

Mindfulness is a powerful tool in overcoming a scarcity mindset. This mindset, characterized by feelings of lack and limitation, often stems from our thoughts and habits rather than actual external constraints. A scarcity mindset can make you feel as though there is never enough time, energy, or resources to accomplish what you need or desire. As a result, you may find yourself stuck in a cycle of stress, procrastination, and time-wasting habits that drain your productivity and sense of well-being.

By practicing mindfulness, you can begin to notice these counterproductive habits and create a more intentional, focused approach to how you spend your time. Mindfulness helps you become aware of your thoughts, emotions, and behaviors in the present moment, allowing you to break free from automatic patterns that contribute to a scarcity mindset. One of the key ways mindfulness can help is by enabling you to catch time-wasting habits and schedule focused time for tasks, thus promoting productivity and a sense of abundance.

The Link Between a Scarcity Mindset and Time Management

A scarcity mindset isn't just about money or resources—it often extends to how we perceive and use our time. If you frequently feel like there aren't enough hours in the day to accomplish everything you need to do, you may be operating from a scarcity mindset when it comes to time. This feeling can be exacerbated by stress, multitasking, and a lack of focus, leading to inefficiency and overwhelm.

When we're caught in a scarcity mindset about time, we may engage in time-wasting habits without even realizing it. These can include:

- Procrastination: Putting off important tasks because they feel overwhelming or because you believe there isn't enough time to do them well.

- Distraction: Constantly checking your phone, email, or social media instead of staying focused on the task at hand.

- Multitasking: Trying to juggle multiple tasks at once, which often results in lower-quality work and a longer time to complete each task.

- Perfectionism: Spending excessive amounts of time on minor details, driven by the fear of not being good enough.

These habits create a vicious cycle: the more time we waste, the more pressure we feel, which reinforces the belief that we don't have enough time. Mindfulness can help you break this cycle by bringing awareness to your time-wasting habits and helping you make more conscious, productive choices about how you spend your time.

Step 1: Practice Mindful Awareness of Your Habits

The first step in using mindfulness to combat time-wasting habits is to develop a deeper awareness of how you currently spend your time. Mindfulness is about paying attention to the present moment without judgment, and this includes being honest with yourself about your habits.

Throughout the day, make a conscious effort to observe your thoughts, feelings, and actions. When you find yourself procrastinating, getting distracted, or multitasking, notice what is happening without judgment. Ask yourself:

- What thoughts or feelings are triggering this behavior?

- Am I avoiding a task because it feels too difficult or overwhelming?

- Am I checking my phone or email out of habit, boredom, or anxiety?

- How do I feel when I'm multitasking? Am I truly being productive, or am I just feeling busy?

By practicing this kind of mindful self-awareness, you can start to identify the underlying emotions or thought patterns that lead to time-wasting behaviors. You may notice that feelings of anxiety, fear of failure, or boredom are driving your actions. Once you recognize these patterns, you can begin to make more intentional choices about how you spend your time.

Step 2: Catch Time-Wasting Habits in the Moment

Mindfulness is not just about observing your habits after the fact—it's about learning to catch them in real time. The more you practice mindful awareness, the better you'll become at recognizing when you're slipping into time-wasting habits.

For example, let's say you're working on an important project and suddenly feel the urge to check social media. In that moment, mindfulness can help you pause and ask yourself:

- Why am I reaching for my phone right now?

- Is this a productive use of my time, or am I avoiding the task?

- How will I feel afterward if I indulge in this distraction?

By catching yourself in the act, you can make a conscious decision to either continue with the distraction or refocus on your task. This moment of mindfulness gives you the power to choose, rather than letting your habits control you. Over time, this practice helps you build discipline and reduce the frequency of time-wasting behaviors.

Step 3: Schedule Focused Time for Tasks

One of the most effective ways to combat a scarcity mindset about time is to use mindfulness to plan and structure your day intentionally. Rather than letting your day unfold reactively, schedule specific blocks of time for focused work, using mindfulness to stay present and engaged during these periods.

The practice of time-blocking involves setting aside dedicated time slots for particular tasks or activities. During these time blocks, commit to focusing exclusively on the task at hand, free from distractions. Here's how you can incorporate mindfulness into this practice:

- Set Clear Intentions: At the beginning of each time block, take a moment to set a clear intention for what you want to accomplish. This helps anchor your focus and directs your energy toward your goal. For example, you might set an intention to write a report, respond to emails, or work on a creative project.

- Stay Present: As you work, practice staying fully present with the task. If you notice your mind wandering or the urge to check your phone arises, gently bring your attention back to your work. Use mindfulness to observe these distractions without judgment, and then refocus.

- Take Mindful Breaks: Mindfulness doesn't mean working non-stop. It's important to take breaks to recharge your focus. However, these breaks should be intentional and mindful. Instead of mindlessly scrolling through social media, consider stepping away from your desk, taking a few deep breaths, or practicing a short mindfulness meditation to reset your energy and clarity.

By scheduling focused time for tasks and practicing mindfulness during those time blocks, you create a sense of control over your time. You are no longer at the mercy of distractions or time-wasting habits. Instead, you are making conscious choices about how to use your time effectively.

Step 4: Reflect and Adjust

At the end of each day or week, take time to reflect on how you managed your time and whether you were able to stay mindful and focused. Ask yourself:

- What went well?

- Where did I fall into time-wasting habits?

- What emotions or triggers led to those habits?

- How can I adjust my approach moving forward?

This reflective practice allows you to continually improve your time management and mindfulness skills. By being honest with yourself about your progress, you can make small adjustments that lead to greater productivity and a more abundant mindset.

Conclusion

Practicing mindfulness is an effective way to catch time-wasting habits and take control of your time. By becoming more aware of your thoughts, emotions, and behaviors, you can identify the underlying patterns that lead to procrastination, distraction, and inefficiency. Mindfulness empowers you to break free from a scarcity mindset about time and approach your day with intention and focus.

Through mindful awareness, scheduling focused time blocks, and reflecting on your progress, you can develop habits that promote productivity and a sense of abundance. As you practice mindfulness in your daily life, you'll begin to see that there is enough time to accomplish your goals—when you manage it with awareness and purpose. This shift in perspective can help you overcome the limitations of a scarcity mindset and move toward greater success, fulfillment, and balance.

Design affirmations: Repeat positive affirmations to yourself to override negative thoughts.

Designing Affirmations to Combat a Scarcity Mindset

A scarcity mindset is a deeply ingrained belief system that revolves around lack and limitation. It can manifest as feelings of inadequacy, fear of failure, and a persistent sense that there's never enough—whether it be money, time, opportunities, or personal resources. This mindset can hinder personal growth, decision-making, and overall life satisfaction. However, it's possible to shift from a scarcity mindset to one of abundance through various practices, one of the most powerful being the use of positive affirmations.

Affirmations are positive, self-empowering statements designed to replace negative thought patterns and reshape your beliefs. By repeating these affirmations consistently, you can start to override the deeply rooted negative beliefs that fuel a scarcity mindset. When affirmations are used mindfully, they serve as tools for rewiring the brain, promoting confidence, and instilling a sense of self-worth and abundance. In this discussion, we will explore how to design effective affirmations that target the scarcity mindset and suggest 10 affirmations that you can use to help change this mindset.

The Power of Affirmations in Overcoming Scarcity

Negative self-talk and limiting beliefs are at the core of the scarcity mindset. Thoughts such as "I'm not good enough," "There's never enough to go around," or "I will never succeed" can paralyze action and cause self-doubt. These thoughts create mental blocks that reinforce feelings of lack, which then impact behavior, leading to procrastination, avoidance of risks, and stagnation.

Affirmations counteract these limiting beliefs by encouraging positive thinking and fostering a sense of abundance. Repeated over time, affirmations help reprogram the subconscious mind and gradually shift one's perception of reality. The process of repeating affirmations helps build new neural pathways in the brain, making positive thoughts more automatic. This shift enables you to approach challenges with confidence, recognize opportunities, and feel more in control of your life.

Affirmations work by:

1. Rewriting Negative Thoughts: Negative thoughts often arise from past experiences, limiting beliefs, or societal conditioning. By repeating positive affirmations, you actively counter these negative thoughts and replace them with empowering ones.

2. Boosting Self-Esteem: When you affirm positive statements about yourself and your potential, you start to believe in your abilities. This boosts self-

esteem and encourages you to take action toward your goals.

3. Promoting a Growth Mindset: Affirmations encourage the belief that you are capable of learning, growing, and adapting. This is essential for overcoming a scarcity mindset, which tends to view life as static and unchangeable.

4. Creating Abundance Thinking: Affirmations focused on abundance help shift your perspective from focusing on what you lack to appreciating what you have and recognizing the opportunities available to you.

How to Design Effective Affirmations

Creating affirmations that truly resonate with you is key to making them effective. Here are some guidelines for designing affirmations that specifically target a scarcity mindset:

1. Make Them Personal: Use "I" statements to make the affirmation about you. This personalizes the statement, making it more meaningful and powerful.

2. Keep Them Positive: Ensure your affirmations focus on what you want to bring into your life, rather than what you want to avoid. Avoid using negative words like "don't" or "can't." For example,

instead of saying "I won't fail," say "I am capable of achieving success."

3. Focus on the Present: Use present tense in your affirmations. Rather than saying "I will be successful," say "I am successful." This signals to your brain that abundance is already a part of your reality, helping to shift your mindset in the present moment.

4. Be Specific and Action-Oriented: Tailor your affirmations to address specific areas where you feel scarcity. For example, if you feel you lack time, you might say, "I have enough time to accomplish everything that is important to me."

5. Believe in Your Affirmations: Choose affirmations that you can realistically believe in, even if they stretch your current beliefs. Affirmations should feel empowering and attainable, helping you move toward a growth mindset.

Suggested Affirmations to Overcome a Scarcity Mindset

Here are 10 powerful affirmations that specifically target the scarcity mindset. Use these affirmations to help shift your thinking from lack to abundance:

1. "I am enough, and I have enough."

This affirmation directly combats the feeling of insufficiency, reminding you that who you are and what you have is sufficient.

2. "Opportunities are abundant, and I attract success easily."

This affirmation helps you recognize that there are plenty of opportunities available and that you are capable of attracting them into your life.

3. "I release all fears of not having enough and trust that I am always supported."

Scarcity often stems from fear. This affirmation encourages you to let go of those fears and trust in the process of life.

4. "I am worthy of all the abundance and success that flows into my life."

A scarcity mindset can make you feel unworthy of success. This affirmation helps reaffirm your worth and deservingness.

5. "Every day, I take positive steps toward abundance."

This statement encourages action and growth, reinforcing the idea that abundance comes through consistent, positive effort.

6. "I focus on what I can control and let go of what I cannot."

Often, scarcity thinking involves focusing on things outside of your control. This affirmation reminds you to focus on what you can influence, reducing feelings of helplessness.

7. "I have enough time, energy, and resources to accomplish everything important to me."

Time scarcity is a common feeling. This affirmation helps counteract the belief that there is never enough time by reminding you that you can manage your time effectively.

8. "My thoughts create my reality, and I am the master of my thoughts."

This affirmation empowers you to take control of your mindset and recognize that your thoughts are powerful in shaping your experience of life.

9. "I am open to receiving all the wealth and abundance that the universe has to offer."

Scarcity thinking can block the flow of abundance. This affirmation invites you to be open to receiving more without feeling limited.

10. "I am grateful for all that I have, and I welcome more blessings into my life."

Practicing gratitude is a powerful way to overcome scarcity. This affirmation fosters a mindset of appreciation while welcoming further abundance.

How to Use Affirmations Effectively

To get the most out of affirmations, consistency is key. Here are a few strategies for incorporating affirmations into your daily routine:

1. Repeat Them Daily: Start and end your day by repeating your affirmations. This sets a positive tone for the day and helps reinforce your new mindset before bed.

2. Write Them Down: Writing your affirmations in a journal helps solidify them in your mind and makes them feel more concrete.

3. Speak Them with Conviction: When you say your affirmations, do so with confidence and belief. The more you say them with emotion and sincerity, the more effective they will be.

4. Use Visual Cues: Place your affirmations where you will see them regularly—on your mirror, in your workspace, or as reminders on your phone.

5. Visualize Your Success: As you repeat your affirmations, visualize yourself living in alignment with them. Imagine yourself experiencing the abundance, success, or fulfillment that your affirmations describe.

Conclusion

Designing and using affirmations is a powerful method for overcoming a scarcity mindset. By repeating positive, empowering statements, you can gradually replace limiting beliefs with thoughts that support growth, confidence, and abundance. Affirmations not only help shift your mindset but also encourage you to take action, recognize opportunities, and cultivate a life of fulfillment. Start incorporating these affirmations into your daily routine to begin the transformation from scarcity to abundance.

Collaborate and share: Seek opportunities to collaborate and share your knowledge and skills.

Collaborating and Sharing as a Means to Combat a Scarcity Mindset

A scarcity mindset is rooted in the belief that resources are limited—whether it's time, money, opportunities, or even personal value. This type of thinking can hinder personal growth, professional development, and overall satisfaction in life. It keeps individuals in a cycle of fear, competition, and isolation, believing that if they give something away, they'll have less for themselves. However, one powerful way to overcome a scarcity mindset is to embrace collaboration and sharing. By seeking opportunities to collaborate and share your knowledge and skills, you not only build confidence but also affirm your personal value and resourcefulness. This shift in mindset fosters abundance, personal growth, and mutual success.

The Link Between Scarcity and Isolation

One of the hallmarks of a scarcity mindset is a sense of isolation. People with this mindset often view others as competitors rather than collaborators, leading to a reluctance to share their knowledge or skills. They may fear that sharing will diminish their value, or that helping someone else succeed will reduce their own chances of success. This thinking creates a self-imposed barrier to growth and reinforces the notion that there isn't enough to go around.

The scarcity mindset also fosters a sense of self-preservation, where individuals hoard their resources, knowledge, and even opportunities, believing that this is the only way to protect themselves in a world of limited options. Unfortunately, this isolation only deepens the feelings of lack and insecurity, making it harder to recognize the opportunities that collaboration can bring.

Collaboration as a Path to Abundance

On the flip side, collaboration opens the door to abundance. When you collaborate with others, you tap into a collective pool of knowledge, skills, and resources, far greater than what you have alone.

This sharing of expertise and talents benefits everyone involved. Collaboration fosters creativity, problem-solving, and innovation, allowing individuals to accomplish more together than they ever could individually.

By working together, you learn from others, gain new perspectives, and expand your own capabilities. Collaboration is a reminder that life isn't a zero-sum game—there is plenty of success, opportunities, and resources to go around. This mindset shift is fundamental to moving from scarcity to abundance. Moreover, the act of sharing what you know and contributing your skills affirms your value and helps you see yourself as a resourceful, capable individual who has much to offer.

How Sharing Builds Confidence and
Reinforces Your Value

Sharing your knowledge, skills, and experiences is a powerful way to combat the feelings of inadequacy that often accompany a scarcity mindset. When you share, you reinforce your own expertise and capabilities. Teaching others or collaborating on projects allows you to see the value of what you know and can do, boosting your self-esteem and confidence.

Here's how collaboration and sharing help build confidence and combat a scarcity mindset:

1. Validation of Your Expertise: When you share your knowledge or skills with others, you receive feedback, which often affirms the value of what you bring to the table. Seeing others benefit from your contributions reinforces your self-worth and reminds you that you have something valuable to offer.

2. Learning Through Teaching: The act of teaching or explaining something to others deepens your own understanding. You gain clarity on your strengths and capabilities, and this insight reinforces your confidence. You start to see yourself not as someone who lacks, but as someone who is capable of learning and teaching.

3. Strengthening Relationships: Collaboration fosters relationships built on trust and mutual respect. When you contribute to the success of others, you build connections that can lead to

future opportunities. These relationships serve as a reminder that you are not alone in your journey and that success can be shared and celebrated collectively.

4. Expanding Opportunities: When you collaborate, you gain access to opportunities that might not have been available if you had worked alone. The more you engage in collaborative efforts, the more doors open, whether through networking, referrals, or new projects. This abundance of opportunities helps to dismantle the belief that there is only so much to go around.

5. Affirming Your Resourcefulness: Sharing your knowledge and skills demonstrates that you are resourceful and adaptable. It shows that you have the ability to contribute meaningfully to different situations, which strengthens your belief in your own capability. This belief is essential in shifting

away from a scarcity mindset, where individuals often feel powerless or ineffective.

Strategies for Seeking Collaboration and Sharing

To harness the power of collaboration and sharing in overcoming a scarcity mindset, it's important to intentionally seek out opportunities to work with others and offer your knowledge and skills. Here are some strategies to help you get started:

1. Identify Areas of Strength

Take some time to reflect on your skills, knowledge, and experiences. What do you excel at? What unique insights can you offer others? Once you've identified your strengths, look for opportunities to share them, whether through mentoring, teaching, or collaborating on projects.

2. Join a Community

Surround yourself with like-minded individuals who share your interests or goals. Whether it's joining a professional association, a mastermind group, or an online community, being part of a collective can provide opportunities for collaboration and sharing. Communities offer a platform to contribute your skills, learn from others, and create mutually beneficial relationships.

3. Offer Help and Support

One of the simplest ways to start collaborating is to offer your help. Look for opportunities where you can lend your expertise or skills to others. This could be as simple as offering advice, providing feedback, or volunteering to assist with a project. By giving freely, you create an environment of abundance, where knowledge and resources are shared openly.

4. Seek Out Partnerships

Consider partnering with others on projects or initiatives that align with your goals. Collaboration can take many forms, from co-authoring a paper or blog post to working on a joint business venture. Partnerships allow you to combine your strengths with others, creating a powerful synergy that benefits all parties involved.

5. Embrace a Mindset of Contribution

Shift your focus from what you can get to what you can give. When you approach collaboration with a mindset of contribution, you begin to see how your knowledge and skills can make a difference in others' lives. This mindset of generosity fosters a sense of abundance, as you realize that giving to others doesn't deplete your resources—it enhances them.

Learning from others is another powerful form of collaboration. Seek out peers or mentors who have expertise in areas you want to grow in. By sharing your own insights and learning from others, you not only expand your own knowledge but also strengthen your sense of community and abundance.

Collaboration in the Professional World

In a professional setting, collaboration can be particularly beneficial in overcoming a scarcity mindset. Whether you're in a corporate environment, running your own business, or working in a freelance capacity, collaboration is key to growth and innovation. Professionals who collaborate and share their knowledge with colleagues are often seen as valuable team players, which can lead to new opportunities for advancement.

Collaboration also plays a crucial role in networking. By building relationships based on trust and shared success, you expand your professional circle and increase your visibility. Opportunities, partnerships, and resources become more accessible when you're known as someone who collaborates openly and shares generously.

Conclusion

Collaboration and sharing are transformative practices that can help dismantle a scarcity mindset. By actively seeking opportunities to collaborate and share your knowledge and skills, you not only build confidence and affirm your personal value but also foster an environment of abundance. Rather than competing or hoarding resources, collaboration invites mutual success and growth. As you embrace collaboration, you will begin to see that there is more than enough to go around—both for you and for others—and that together, we can create more than we ever could alone.

Five Key Strategies to Develop a Growth Mindset Powerful Enough to Transform a Scarcity Mindset into an Abundance Mindset

A scarcity mindset traps people in a cycle of limitation and fear, where they believe resources—whether material, emotional, or intellectual—are finite. This mentality often manifests as self-doubt, fear of failure, and a sense that there's never enough, whether it be time, money, or opportunities.

In contrast, an abundance mindset thrives on the belief that there is more than enough to go around. By developing a growth mindset, which embraces learning, adaptability, and potential, you can shift from scarcity thinking to abundance thinking. Here are five key strategies that can help you transform a scarcity mindset into an abundance mindset.

1. Embrace Challenges as Opportunities for Growth

One of the core principles of a growth mindset is the belief that challenges are not threats but opportunities to learn and grow. People with a scarcity mindset tend to avoid challenges because they fear failure or believe they lack the necessary skills to succeed. However, individuals with a growth mindset see challenges as stepping stones that bring them closer to their goals.

To cultivate this mindset, it's essential to reframe how you view difficulties. Instead of seeing challenges as obstacles, view them as opportunities to develop new skills, gain experience, and grow as a person. For example, if you face a challenge at work, such as learning a new system or leading a project, rather than focusing on what could go wrong, focus on what you can learn from the experience.

Practical steps to embrace challenges include:

- Start Small: Take on manageable challenges that push you slightly out of your comfort zone. As you succeed in these smaller tasks, you'll build the confidence to tackle bigger ones.

- Focus on Learning, Not Results: Instead of measuring success by whether you win or lose, focus on the knowledge and experience you gain from the process.

- Celebrate Progress: Acknowledge your improvements, no matter how small, as they represent growth.

By embracing challenges, you unlock new possibilities and opportunities that help you shift from scarcity to abundance thinking.

2. Shift from Fixed Beliefs to Growth-Oriented Beliefs

A scarcity mindset is often driven by fixed beliefs. People with a fixed mindset believe that their abilities, intelligence, and talents are set in stone, and there is little they can do to change them. In contrast, a growth mindset revolves around the belief that abilities can be developed through dedication, effort, and continuous learning.

To foster a growth mindset, start by challenging your own fixed beliefs. For example, if you believe you're "not good at math," recognize that this belief may be limiting your potential. With the right mindset, you can improve your skills through practice and learning.

Here are strategies to shift from fixed beliefs to growth-oriented beliefs:

- Identify Limiting Beliefs: Pay attention to your internal dialogue and identify any fixed beliefs you hold about yourself. Common fixed beliefs include "I'm not smart enough" or "I'm not creative."

- Challenge Your Assumptions: Once you identify these limiting beliefs, question whether they are truly accurate. Ask yourself, "Is there evidence that I can improve in this area?"

- Adopt a Learning Mindset: Replace fixed thoughts with growth-oriented ones. For example, instead of saying, "I'm not good at public speaking," shift to "I can become better at public speaking with practice and feedback."

Over time, you'll start to see that your potential isn't fixed, and that growth is possible in any area, shifting your mindset toward abundance.

3. Practice Gratitude and Focus on What You Have

Gratitude is a powerful antidote to a scarcity mindset. When you focus on what you have, you begin to realize that you are not lacking as much as you might have believed. This shift in focus helps you cultivate an abundance mindset by recognizing the blessings and opportunities already present in your life.

Gratitude practices can include:

- Gratitude Journaling: At the end of each day, write down three things you're grateful for. These can be simple things, such as a kind gesture from a friend, a good meal, or an achievement at work.

- Acknowledge Small Wins: Celebrate small accomplishments and moments of joy, as they are indicators of abundance in your life.

- Shift Your Focus: When you catch yourself thinking about what you lack, redirect your focus to what you already have. For example, if you're worried about not having enough time, focus on how you've effectively used your time in the past or the time you have right now to take action.

Gratitude not only shifts your perspective but also boosts your confidence and resourcefulness, helping you to feel that life offers more than enough to meet your needs.

4. Surround Yourself with Positive, Growth-Oriented People

The people you spend time with have a significant impact on your mindset. If you surround yourself with individuals who constantly focus on what they lack, it can reinforce your own scarcity mindset. Conversely, surrounding yourself with people who embody a growth and abundance mindset can inspire you to think differently.

Growth-oriented individuals are often optimistic, solution-focused, and open to new ideas. They see possibilities where others see limitations and are willing to invest in learning and self-improvement. By spending time with people who embrace this mindset, you can learn from their perspectives and adopt their positive habits.

Here are some ways to surround yourself with growth-oriented people:

- Join Communities of Learners: Look for groups, clubs, or networks where people are dedicated to personal and professional growth. This could be a mastermind group, a learning circle, or a professional association.

- Seek Out Mentors: Find mentors who have a growth mindset and can guide you through challenges with wisdom and encouragement.

- Limit Negative Influences: Be mindful of the people who consistently focus on negativity or limitations. While it's important to support friends and loved ones, consider creating some distance from those who consistently reinforce a scarcity mindset.

By cultivating relationships with positive, growth-minded individuals, you'll be exposed to new ways of thinking and feel more supported in your efforts to develop an abundance mindset.

5. Take Consistent Action and Celebrate Progress

The key to developing a growth mindset is not just in thinking differently but also in taking action. People with a scarcity mindset often hesitate to take risks or pursue new opportunities because they fear failure or believe they don't have enough resources. However, growth comes from taking consistent action, even if it means stepping into uncertainty.

To develop a growth mindset, make a habit of taking small, incremental steps toward your goals. These actions don't need to be perfect—they just need to move you forward. Over time, these small actions will build momentum, helping you see that progress is always possible.

Strategies for taking consistent action include:

- Set Small, Achievable Goals: Break down big goals into smaller, manageable tasks. This makes it easier to start and maintain momentum.

- Track Your Progress: Keep a record of your accomplishments, no matter how small. Tracking progress reinforces the belief that you are capable of growth.

- Celebrate Wins Along the Way: Don't wait for a major milestone to celebrate. Acknowledge every step forward, as each one represents growth and success.

By taking action and celebrating your progress, you'll start to shift your focus from what you don't have to what you're capable of achieving, reinforcing an abundance mindset.

Conclusion

Developing a growth mindset is essential for transforming a scarcity mindset into one of abundance. By embracing challenges, shifting from fixed beliefs to growth-oriented thinking, practicing gratitude, surrounding yourself with positive influences, and taking consistent action, you can break free from limiting thoughts and unlock a world of possibilities.

The journey from scarcity to abundance is not about acquiring more material wealth—it's about realizing that growth, learning, and opportunities are endless when you adopt a mindset of abundance.

RECAP

Transforming a scarcity mindset into an abundance mindset is like tending a garden. A scarcity mindset plants seeds of fear, limiting beliefs, and self-doubt, which choke potential growth. To shift toward abundance, you must systematically pull out those weeds to plant and nurture seeds of growth.

First, embrace challenges as opportunities for learning, like sunlight that helps you grow stronger with each struggle. Challenge fixed beliefs, as if you're replanting your mindset in fertile soil, knowing your abilities can blossom with effort.

Practicing gratitude is like watering the garden—it may not be the biggest garden, but what was once just dirt and seeds is now bringing nourishment and life. Acknowledging what you already have helps abundance thinking thrive.

Surround yourself with positive people who nourish your growth like companions in the garden, sharing their wisdom and encouragement as they watch and cheer mutual growth.

Finally, taking consistent action is the daily care that turns small steps into flourishing progress. You tend to your garden daily, with small deliberate actions having confidence the smallest of tasks will gave a profound effect in time. Celebrate every win as if watching each new flower bloom, and knowing it is just a prelude until the next success.

With these five strategies—embracing challenges, shifting beliefs, practicing gratitude, connecting with growth-oriented people, and taking consistent action—you can cultivate a mindset of abundance. Like a well-tended garden, a growth mindset brings endless potential, where you no longer see limits but instead recognize the fertile ground of opportunity all around you.

Be forever inspired to to nourish your mindset with positivity and watch it flourish.